# The Singing Bird

Story retold by Monica Hughes
Pictures by Lucy Truman

There was once a little bird. She sang a lot. Everyone was happy.

The king saw the little bird.

He said, "Come and live in this lovely cage."

"Sing little bird!" said the king.
The little bird did not sing.
She was too sad.

Then the king said, “Here is some food for you.”

“Now, sing little bird, sing.”

But the little bird did not sing. She was very sad. Now the king was very sad, too.

Then the king let the bird out.
“Go little bird, go!” he said.

She went up and up and up.

Then the little bird was happy.
She sang and sang and
everyone was happy.

The king was very
happy, too.